A Tale of Two Cities

Charles Dickens

NOW AGE BOOKS
ILLUSTRATED

Pendulum Press, Inc.

West Haven, Connecticut

ISBN 0-88301-093-3 Complete Set
0-88301-134-4 This Volume

Published by
Pendulum Press, Inc.
An Academic Industries, Inc. Company
The Academic Building
Saw Mill Road
West Haven, Connecticut 06516

Printed in the United States of America

TO THE TEACHER

Pendulum Press is proud to offer the NOW AGE ILLUSTRATED Series to schools throughout the country. This completely new series has been prepared by the finest artists and illustrators from around the world. The script adaptations have been prepared by professional writers and revised by qualified reading consultants.

Implicit in the development of the Series are several assumptions. Within the limits of propriety, anything a child reads and/or wants to read is *per se* an educational tool. Educators have long recognized this and have clamored for materials that incorporate this premise. The sustained popularity of the illustrated format, for example, has been documented, but it has not been fully utilized for educational purposes. Out of this realization, the NOW AGE ILLUSTRATED Series evolved.

In the actual reading process, the illustrated panel encourages and supports the student's desire to read printed words. The combination of words and picture helps the student to a greater understanding of the subject; and understanding, that comes from reading, creates the desire for more reading.

The final assumption is that reading as an end in itself is self-defeating. Children are motivated to read material that satisfies their quest for knowledge and understanding of their world. In this series, they are exposed to some of the greatest stories, authors, and characters in the English language. The Series will stimulate their desire to read the original edition when their reading skills are sufficiently developed. More importantly, reading books in the NOW AGE ILLUSTRATED Series will help students establish a mental "pegboard" of information – images, names, and concepts – to which they are exposed. Let's assume, for example, that a child sees a television commercial which features Huck Finn in some way. If he has read the NOW AGE Huck Finn, the TV reference has meaning for him which gives the child a surge of satisfaction and accomplishment.

After using the NOW AGE ILLUSTRATED editions, we know that you will share our enthusiasm about the series and its concept.

–The Editors

ABOUT THE AUTHOR

The most popular, and perhaps the greatest of English novelists was Charles Dickens. Born in 1812, Dickens was the son of a clerk in the Navy-Pay office.

Although from a poor background, Dickens was both ambitious and industrious. His education came from books, those in school as well as his own. He wrote of people as he saw them and created some of the most timeless characters in literature.

The turning point in his life came at the time of his marriage. Both his wedding day and his first publication occurred in the same year. From that time, he continued to write many novels during the conventional Victorian era.

One of his most famous works is *A Tale of Two Cities.* This novel is a serious and sensational experiment in historical romance. It has a dual theme: love and death, and what effect they have on the novel's characters.

Charles Dickens
A Tale of Two Cities

Adapted by
NAUNERLE FARR

Illustrated by
ALFREDO P. ALCALA

a
VINCENT FAGO
production

Sydney Carton
Dr. Manette
Charles Darnay
Madame Defarge
Lucie Manette
Mr. Lorry
Miss Pross
Monsieur Defarge

Until the year 1775, the kings of both France and England ruled with great power. But they did not rule kindly or fairly, and people all over were dying from hunger. At last the peasants of France, some 300,000 in number, joined together to overthrow the King. They captured him, tried him, found him guilty, and had him beheaded.

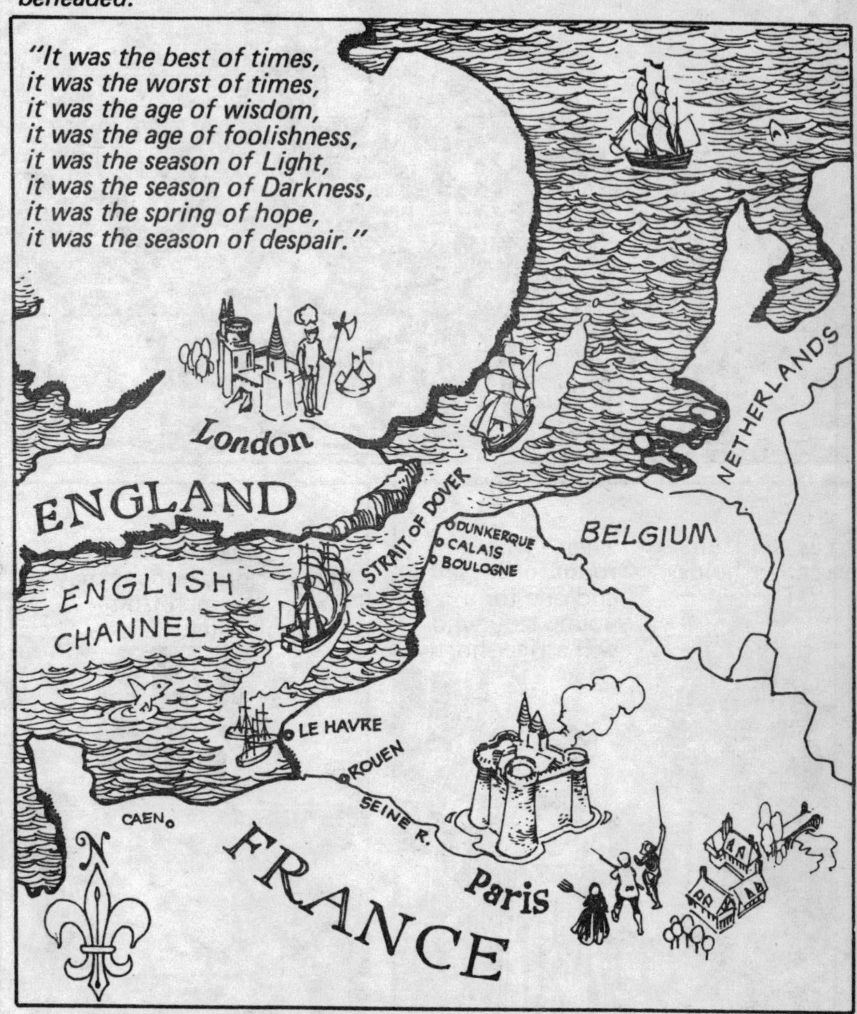
"It was the best of times,
it was the worst of times,
it was the age of wisdom,
it was the age of foolishness,
it was the season of Light,
it was the season of Darkness,
it was the spring of hope,
it was the season of despair."
London
ENGLAND
ENGLISH CHANNEL
STRAIT OF DOVER
DUNKERQUE
CALAIS
BOULOGNE
BELGIUM
NETHERLANDS
LE HAVRE
ROUEN
SEINE R.
CAEN
N
FRANCE
Paris

It is at this time that our story takes place. . .set in the cities of Paris and London. . .the people are some of the innocent and some of the guilty who were alive at that time.

One winter day in 1775, the mail coach from London finished its journey to Dover.

Welcome, sir! A room?

Will there be a boat to Calais* tomorrow?

Yes, sir, if the weather holds.
Then I wish a room for myself—and one for a young lady who will arrive shortly.

She may ask for me by name—Lorry—or she may ask for the man from Tellson's Bank.

* a city in France

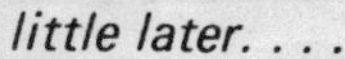
little later. . . .

Miss Manette has
rrived, sir.
So soon?

The Bank writes there is news about my poor dead father—that I must go to Paris. May I go with you?
I would be pleased, Ma'am.

hey said you
vould have
urprising news
or me and that
ou would
xplain.
Well. . .it is hard to begin!

Twenty years ago in Paris I did some work for a Frenchman, a famous doctor. . .Dr. Manette.
My father!

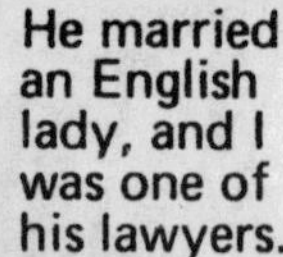
He married an English lady, and I was one of his lawyers.

My mother outlived my father by only two years—then I was left an orphan. . . .
Was it you who brought me to England?
It was I. And now suppose—that your fathe had not died!

Suppose he had been taken away by an enemy—that he had been secretly put in prison. . . .

That his wife had begged the King and the court, for news of him, but she never was answered.

The truth—I beg you!
My dear, he has been found. He is alive!

It will be his ghost!
No! Greatly changed, worn out, but alive, and taken to the house of an old servant in Paris.

We will go to him there: —I to prove who he is; and you to bring him back to life!

In the St. Antoine area of Paris, on a narrow, dirty street, was the wine shop of M. and Mme. Defarge. Mr. Lorry took Lucie there upon their arrival in Paris.

M. Defarge?

Sit down. My husband will be here soon.

M. Defarge entered the shop smiling, open-faced.

We came to see Dr. Manette.
Good day. May I help you?

He led them into an apartment, up a steep, dark dirty staircase with garbage on every landing.

Best to start slowly. It is five flights up.

When he learned who Mr. Lorry was, he was changed instantly into an angry man.

This way, please.

He stopped at the door of an attic room and took out a key.

He has lived so long locked up, he would be afraid if the door were left open.
Is it possible?

Possible? Yes. And many other such things are possible, and done—done! Every day!

One would have said the attic room was too dark for work; yet a man sat on a low bench, very busy making shoes.

Good day.

You have a visitor.
Dr. Manette, do you remember me?

For a second it looked as if he might remember.

Then darkness fell again. With a deep sigh, he returned to work.

Do you know him?
Yes; for a moment I saw the face I once knew!

He learned shoemaking in prison. He knows nothing else, not even his name, and calls himself by his cell number.

What is your name, sir?
105, North Tower.

Lucie stepped near Dr. Manette.

What—who are you?
Oh, sir! Oh, my dear!

That voice—this golden hair—the same as. . . .But no, you are too young, how can it be? What is your name, my gentle angel?

At another time you shall know my name.

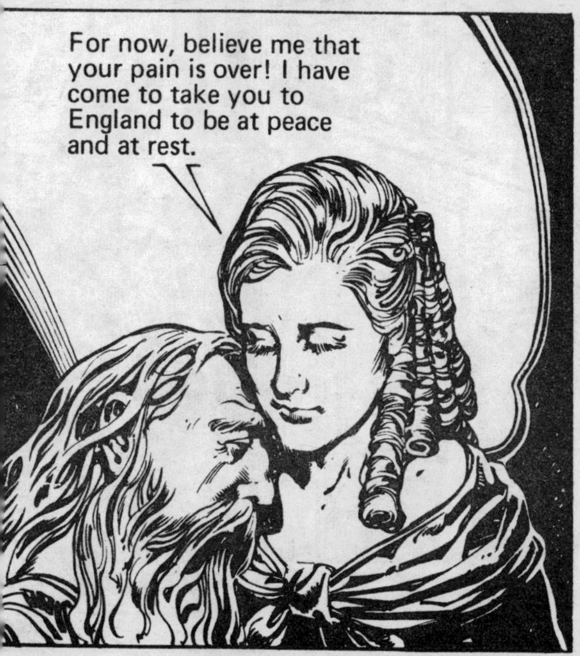
For now, believe me that your pain is over! I have come to take you to England to be at peace and at rest.

So, by coach and by ship, Dr. Manette was taken to London. Slowly, Lucie's tender care brought him back to health. They lived quietly and happily in a pleasant house just off Soho square, where Dr. Manette's medical knowledge and skill brought him many patients.

Five years passed. Then, in 1780, there was great excitement in London over the trial for treason of Charles Darnay, a young Frenchman.*

Found guilty, he'll be!
Cut up and beheaded!
Dead before he'll know what's happened to him!

The prisoner was charged with traveling between England and France to give English secrets to the French King.

I say you are a traitor to our Lord the King of England!

I am not guilty!

* giving secrets to the enemy

The court's lawyer claimed that the proof went back as far as five years. Miss Lucie Manette was called as a witness.

Yes, Mr. Darnay was aboard ship when I brought my ill father from France to London.

He was very kind and gentle and helped to care for my father. I hope I do him no harm today.

The court's lawyer called another witness, a man who was once a servant of Darnay's.

My master often traveled between France and England.

I saw important looking lists and papers in his pockets and in his desk.
Sometimes I saw him show such lists to Frenchmen!

Darnay's lawyer said that his travels were on personal business. Then he asked the servant questions.

Weren't you angry because Mr. Darnay had fired you—for stealing a silver coffee pot?
No, sir! Never!

It was only a little pitcher—and not real silver.
Ha!

Another witness said that he had seen Darnay collecting information near a military post.

Are you quite sure it was the prisoner?
Quite sure!

Look at the gentleman, my assistant. Then look at the prisoner.

The assistant, Sydney Carton, rose and removed his white wig.

They are very like each other!

Can you still be so sure it was the prisoner you saw?

Not only the witness, but everyone present, was surprised by the likeness. The jury found Charles Darnay innocent, and he was released. His friends gathered to congratulate him.

We congratulate you, sir, on your escape from death!

I hope Miss Lucie wasn't too uncomfortable in court.

As father and daughter left, Sydney Carton walked up to Darnay.

It was a strange chance that threw us together. Shall we dine together at the nearest tavern?

Yes, and I owe you thanks for your help today!

I hardly seem to belong to this world again.
My greatest desire is to forget that I belong to it. It has no good in it for me—except wine like this!

I care for no man on earth, and no man cares for me.
That is too bad.

Maybe so. Don't look so happy. You don't know what may come later.
Good night!

Left alone, Carton picked up a candle and went to a mirror on the wall.

Ah! Do you like what you see?

Say it plainly! You hate the fellow—for showing what you once were, and what you might have been.

He returned to his wine, drank it all in a few minutes, and fell asleep on his arms.

Charles Darnay made his home in England, as a teacher of the French language. A part of his time was spent at Cambridge teaching university students. But family business still forced him to make visits to France.

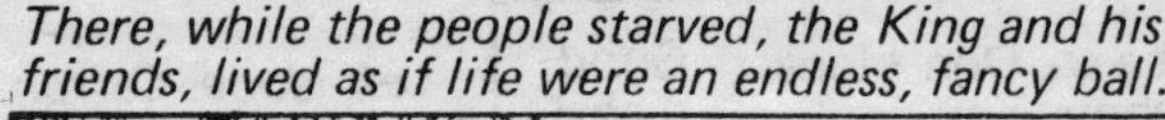

There, while the people starved, the King and his friends, lived as if life were an endless, fancy ball.

Quickly driving through the narrow streets, the rich seemed to enjoy watching the common people jump to escape being run down.

Watch out!

One day as the carriage of the Marquis St. Evremonde swept round a corner, it hit something and the horses reared.

What is wrong? Why does he make that awful noise?
What a pity. It is his child.
Dead! Killed!
Defarge
VIN

Why can't you take care of
your children? I don't know
what injury you have done
to my horses.

The Marquis tossed a gold coin from the window.

Here. Give
him that.

Suddenly the coin flew back through the window.

Wait! Who
threw that?

You dogs! I would
ride over any of you
willingly and wipe you
from the earth.

At sunset, the Marquis arrived at his country estate. Waiting for him was his nephew. Known in England as Charles Darnay, he was the son of the dead twin brother of the Marquis.

You have taken a long time to return.
I only return because I must!

Our family hurts everyone who comes between us and our wishes. Our name is the most hated in France!
It is only natural they should hate us.
Cognac

I am stuck with a way of life I hate! If this property were mine I would give it up, as I have given up France.

It is not yet ycurs! For myself, I will die to protect my power and property!

What is that noise? Open the blinds.

There is nothing here.

Very well. Now I will say good night.
Good night, sir.

Later, as the Marquis slept. . . .

DRIVE HIM
FAST TO
HIS TOMB!

The father of the dead child had his revenge.

Charles Darnay returned to London. There, like a ship safely in harbor after a stormy voyage, Dr. Manette lived in peace with Lucie. The good Miss Pross, with whom Lucie had lived while she was an orphan, was a part of the household. And their friends were always welcome there.

Mr. Lorry, Charles Darnay, and Sydney Carton visited often.

How cool and pleasant it is here.
Not a quieter spot in London.

One day Darnay called when he knew he would find Dr. Manette alone.

Charles Darnay! I am happy to see you.
I wish to speak with you, sir. . . .

I love your daughter with all my heart. I wish to marry her.
I am not surprised!

Have you spoken of this to Lucie?
No, never.

If Lucie should tell me that she needs you for her happiness, I will give her to you.
Thank you, sir!

I must tell you my real name—and why I am in England.
No, stop!

If Lucie loves you, if you marry her, you shall tell me on your wedding day. Not before!

And so it was that Charles Darnay asked Lucie to marry him.

It is with your father's permission that I ask!
Dear Charles, yes!

Soon after it was another man, Sydney Carton, who spoke to Lucie of love.

I do not ask for your love Miss Manette—nor even want it. I am a wasted man who would pull you down with me.

Even without it, can I not help you? Oh, Mr. Carton, think again! Try again!
It is too late. I ask only that you will think kindly of me in your heart.

I will, Mr. Carton, always.
For you, and any dear to you, I would do anything. I would give my life to keep a life you love beside you. God bless you!

The wedding day arrived. Behind the closed door of Dr. Manette's room, Darnay talked with him.

Doctor, it is my mother's name I use. I am truly the Marquis St. Evremonde.

Dr. Manette's face turned pale.

You say. . .St. Evremonde?

Yes. . .is something wrong?
No, no. Go on.

I have given up my rights. I have left my property in the hands of an employee, to be used for the people.

I earn my own living by my own labor.
Yes, I see.

I ask one thing: promise me you will never tell anyone else your true name.
I promise you, sir.

And so Lucie and Charles were married.

Take her, Charles! She is yours!

In Paris, an Englishman, an old friend, came to the Defarge's shop to drink wine.

It was you who cared for Dr. Manette when he was released.
That is true. . . .

Do you know his daughter has married a Frenchman?
No. . . .

He is called Darnay in England, but he is truly the Marquis St. Evremonde!

If it is true, I hope for her sake, Fate will keep her husband out of France.

Her husband's luck will take him where he is to go, and will lead him to the end that is to end him!

n London, Darnay and Lucie lived happily with Dr. Manette. A aughter, little Lucie, lived with them.

I came to see my little Lucie.
You are her favorite, Mr. Carton!

ate on a night in mid-July, 1789, Mr. Lorry came to the Darnay's rom Tellson's Bank.

I began to think I must stay the night at the bank! There is such uneasiness in Paris. Everyone is sending us their property.

That has a bad look.

It is a wild, hot, stormy night.

I have felt uneasy all day.

Yes, there is something strange in the air—like trouble about to begin.

It was July 14. Paris had become like a whirlpool of boiling water. Someone was giving out weapons.

The center of the whirlpool was Defarge's wine shop.

Let's separate and all lead as many men as we can.

And you, my wife?
Defarge! I will lead the women! We can kill as well as the men!

Come then! We are ready! To the Bastille!

With a roar of anger, with alarm bells ringing, drums beating, the crowd attacked the Bastille—the state-prison in Paris, most hated by the people.

The white flag of surrender appeared. The mob swept over the lowered drawbridge into the courtyard, Defarge leading.

Free the prisoners! Go to the secret cells!
You! Take me to 105, North Tower.

In the cell, Defarge examined the walls.

Pass that torch along these walls.

A.M.! Dr. Alexandre Manette! This is it!
AM

Finding a crowbar, he turned to the chimney.

They are here—the papers!

Once begun, the revolution swept over France and became a time of terror. Treated badly for too long, the common people turned upon the King and his friends hurting the innocent along with the guilty. Many rich people fled to England.

Their meeting place in London was Tellson's Bank. There, in August, 1792, Charles Darnay talked to Mr. Lorry.

Must you go to Paris, sir? The city may not be safe.

My dear, Charles, it is safe enough for me.

It is you Frenchmen who stand in danger of being beheaded!

It is very important for the bank that I go, and go tonight!

By the way, here is a letter secretly brought to us from France, but I can't locate the person to whom it should go.
Let me see it.

It was addressed to himself! But Darnay remembered his promise to Dr. Manette not to tell his name.

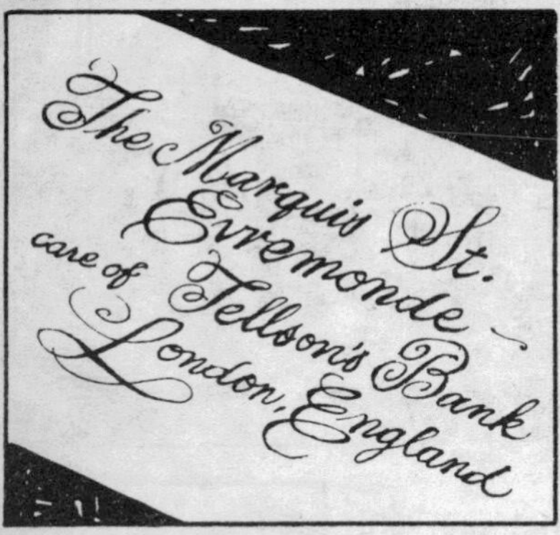
The Marquis St. Evremonde
care of Tellson's Bank
London, England

Later, Darnay read the letter.

Abbaye Prison, Paris
June 21, 1792

Monsieur the Marquis:

I have been seized and imprisoned and shall lose my life, without your help! I am accused of acting against the people for an emigrant.* In vain I say I have acted for the people, according to your commands. They say I have acted for an emigrant, and where is that emigrant?

I beg you to return and release me. I have been true to you, Sir. I pray you to be true to me.

Your unhappy servant
Gabelle

* a person who has left France for safety during the revolution

I know him. I will deliver it. And good luck on your journey.
Goodbye, Charles.

Poor Gabelle! I should not have left him alone to handle things. In my happiness here, I have forgotten my duties in France. I must go to Paris.

I will explain to Lucie and her father in letters to be delivered after I leave. It will keep them from having to say sad goodbyes.

Reaching France, Darnay found things worse than he had expected. Every town gate had its citizen-guards who stopped all those who tried to pass through.

I want to go to Paris!
Emigrant. I am going to send you to Paris with a guard.

In Paris, he was taken before an officer of the people, Citizen Defarge.

You are the emigrant Evremonde?
I am no emigrant, and I am in France of my own free will!

Why, in the name of that sharp thing called La Guillotine*, did you return to France?

You will be held in La Force prison.
Under what law?

We have new laws since you were here.

But have I not the right to. . . .
Emigrants have no rights.

* a machine for beheading persons

A few days later, as Mr. Lorry worked in the Paris office of Tellson's Bank, his door burst open.

Lucie! Dr. Manette! What has brought you here?

Charles is here! An act of kindness brought him, unknown to us. He was stopped at the barrier and sent to La Force prison.
La Force!

My dears, don't worry. I am a Bastille prisoner. Any fighter in France will help me! I know I can help Charles out of danger.
If that is so, act quickly! There is no time to waste! I will keep the others here.

Mr. Lorry knew though the others did not that even at that moment mobs were putting the rich into prisons and killing them by the hundreds.

But Dr. Manette was right. As soon as he made himself known, the crowd took him to its heart and set out to help him.

Make way for the Bastille prisoner! Help the Bastille prisoner's relative. Save the prisoner Evremonde at La Force!

At La Force, he was taken before a committee that was trying the prisoners. One of its members was Defarge. He knew the doctor.

My son-in-law is a prisoner here. I beg you for his life and liberty.
We cannot release him, but we will keep him in safety.

Dr. Manette!
I am going to stay with you—to see that no harm or bad luck finds you turned over to the mob outside!

For four days Dr. Manette stayed with Charles. The next night he was able to send Lucie a note from Charles.

Monsieur Defarge, I believe? And Madame!
Yes, I come from Dr. Manette. I bring a message.

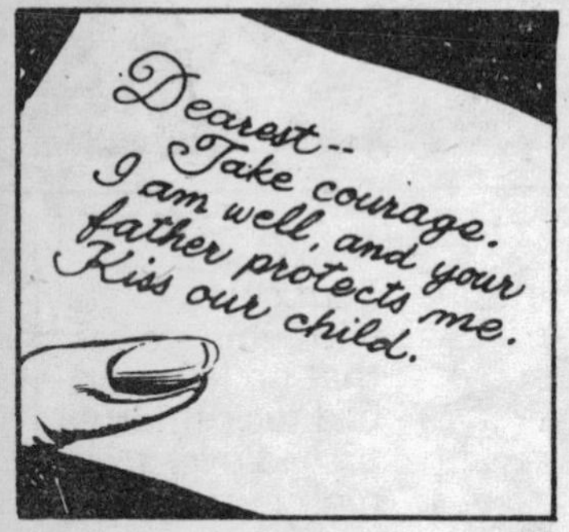
Dearest--
Take courage.
I am well, and your father protects me.
Kiss our child.

He is safe! Oh, thank you, Madame!
Is that Evremonde's child?

Come, Defarge. I have seen them. We may go.

After the Defarges left. . . .

That woman seems to throw a shadow on me and all my hopes!

The worst danger over, Dr. Manette returned. Fifteen months passed. During all that time Lucie was never sure, from hour to hour, whether the Guillotine would strike off her husbands's head next day.

At long last, Charles Darnay was brought to Court. For a second time he stood on trial for his life.

Darnay noticed only two faces in the crowd:

a hard faced woman. . . .

. . . .and his kind father-in-law.

You are accused of being an emigrant, under the law which says all emigrants must stay out of the country forever under. . . .
I do not think of myself as an emigrant, sir.

Have you not lived many years in England?
Yes, sir.

By my own wish I gave up a title and a position I disliked, and went to England to live by my own labors, rather than staying to live on the labors of the people of France!

Did you not marry in England?
True, but I married a French woman.

Her name and family?
Lucie Manette, only daughter of Dr. Manette, the good doctor who sits there.

Darnay was asked why he had returned to France when he did, and Gabelle, who had been freed a few days earlier, spoke for him.

It is true—I wrote and begged him to return to save me!

Then Dr. Manette was questioned.

Darnay has been faithful to my daughter and myself in our exile*.

We have had enough. We are ready to vote.

Every vote was in Darnay's favor.

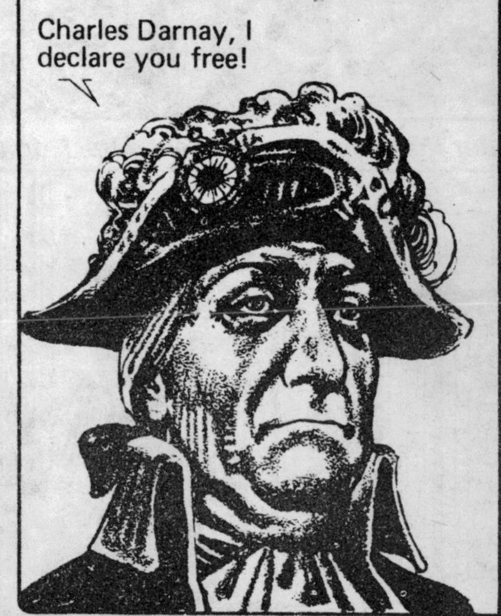
Charles Darnay, I declare you free!

* to live away from one's own country

In a wild, dreamlike parade the crowd carried Darnay home on its shoulders. So, at last, he was back with his family.

Lucie! My own! I am safe.

Now speak to your father. No other man in all France could have done what he has done for me!
Oh, father!
My dear, I am thankful.

But that evening there was a knock on the door.

What can this be! Hide Charles. Save him!
My child, I have saved him. Let me go to the door.

Four armed men in red caps entered the room.

We come to arrest the citizen Evremonde, called Darnay.

How and why am I again a prisoner?
You have been accused by the Section of St. Antoine.

By citizen* and citizeness Defarge—and one other.
What other?

Do you ask, citizen Doctor?
Yes.

Then you will be answered at the trial tomorrow.

* title given to every man and woman in the revolution in France

Sydney Carton had just arrived in Paris and was worried about his friends.

I have bad news. Darnay has been arrested again.
But I left him safe and free only a few hours ago!

I learned of his arrest from a prison spy who owes me something.
Can this man help?

He hasn't much power. But if the trial goes badly, I can make one visit to Darnay in his cell.

Leaving, Carton made his way to a small chemist's shop.

You know the danger if you mix these?
I know.

During the night, knowing he would not sleep, Sydney Carton walked the streets of Paris. He remembered his mother who died in his childhood. He remembered his father's funeral. He walked with purpose, like a man who had found his road and saw its end.

At dawn he stood on a bridge over the river. He watched the stars fade, the sun rise. He remembered the words spoken over his father's grave.

"I am the resurrection and the life; he that believeth in me, though dead, yet shall he live. . . ."*

That morning, again, Darnay was brought to trial.

Charles Evremonde, you are an accused enemy of the French Republic, one of a family of cruel leaders who should die.

Who does the accusing?
Ernest Defarge. Therese Defarge, his wife.

And one other, Alexandre Manette, the doctor.

* words spoken by Christ to his friends

Pale and trembling, Dr. Manette rose.

I protest to you that this is a lie! Who and where is the man who says that I accuse the husband of my child?

Citizen, listen to what follows. In the meantime, be silent.

Defarge spoke. He told of Dr. Manette's imprisonment, of his release, of the Defarge's care of him. He told of the fall of the Bastille, of his visit to cell 105, North Tower; of the hole in the chimney, and the written papers he found there.

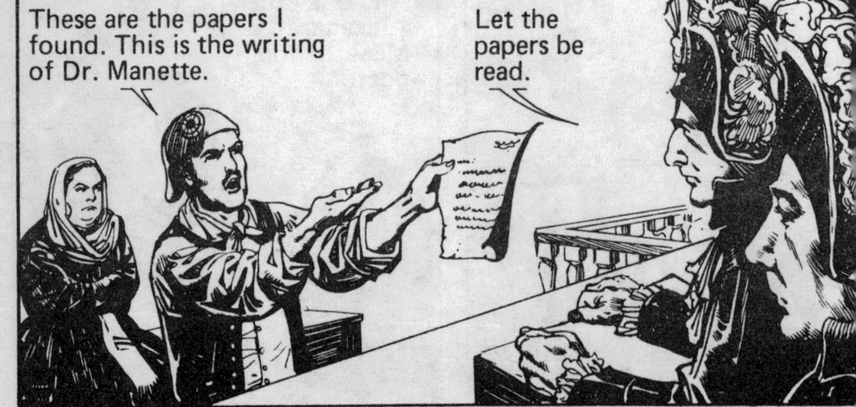
These are the papers I found. This is the writing of Dr. Manette.
Let the papers be read.

I, Alexandre Manette, write this sad paper in my Bastille cell, in the last month of 1767.

I swear that I write the truth. Someone may find it when I and my sorrows are dust.

One night in December, 1757, as I walked by the river, a fast-driven carriage came up behind. I stood aside, but instead of passing, it stopped.

Stop, driver!

Two young men got out. They looked like twin brothers.

You are Dr. Manette?
I am.
Please enter my carriage.

They were armed. I had no choice. I entered and was driven to a lonely country house.

Your patient is upstairs, doctor.

The patient was a beautiful young woman. She was out of her head.

My husband, my father, and my brother!
She has a high fever of the brain.

My husband, my father, my brother!
I fear there is little to do for her.
Very well. There is another patient.

In a loft over a stable, the young woman's brother lay dying of a sword wound.

How did this happen?
He is a common farmer. He forced my brother to draw his sword, and fell by it, like a gentleman.

The boy was dying. He told me his story.

We rented farm land from the Marquis. We were taxed without mercy, worked without mercy, worked without pay. We were robbed and hunted and starved.

They worked my sister's husband to death. Then they took her to the Chateau*. My father died of sorrow.

I took my younger sister to safety. Then I came here. Now I die, too.

* large country home

With a great effort, the boy raised himself.

Marquis, in the days when these crimes will be answered for, I call you and all your family to answer for them!

So the boy died; and shortly afterward, his sister.

Returning home, I wrote a letter to the police telling them the truth of what had happened. But my letter never reached them.

So! You would have told my secret to the police! You will pay for this!

So I was brought to my living grave.

The name of these brothers was Evremonde. I denounce them and their descendants, to the last of their race. I denounce them to Heaven and to Earth.

When the document was finished, a great cry for blood arose in the Court. Every juryman voted "guilty."

To the guillotine!
Guilty!
Guilty!
Guilty!
For you, Charles Evremonde, enemy of the people, death within twenty-four hours!

As Darnay was led away. . . .

I beg your forgiveness.

Never kneel to me! I now know what you felt when you learned my name. With all my heart I thank you for all you have done for me.

But Sydney Carton had made his plans. He went to Defarge's wine shop.

An Englishman—but how like Evremonde!

They were still excited about the trial.

Evremonde is done for, but his wife, and the child—they too must be killed!
We must stop somewhere.

That farm family so hurt by the Evremondes was my family! That boy was my brother. That girl was my sister. That father was my father!

Those dead are my dead!

Tell the Wind and the Fire to stop; not me!

Carton went next to Mr. Lorry's.

My bench—where is it? I must finish the shoes!
Poor fellow! The shock was too much for him.

Carton told what he heard at the wine shop. . .that Lucie and the child were in danger, that Madame Defarge planned to have them killed.

You must take Dr. Manette, Lucie, and the child back to London tomorrow—while their passes to leave are still good.
It shall be done!

Take my pass. Bring the Manettes and meet me outside the prison gates at two o'clock tomorrow. When I come, take me in and drive away for London.

Promise that when my place in the coach is filled, you will let nothing stop you!
I promise.

The following day, in Darnay's cell. . . .

Carton! How—why are you here?

Never mind! Take off your boots and put on mine.

There is no escaping from here—it's madness!

As Darnay removed his coat, Carton knocked him out with the drug he had bought.

In a moment, Darnay was out cold. Carton quickly finished changing their clothing, then called the prison spy.

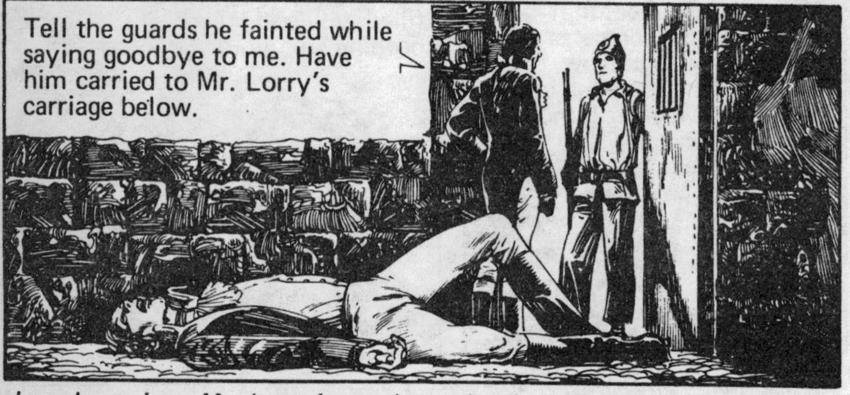
Tell the guards he fainted while saying goodbye to me. Have him carried to Mr. Lorry's carriage below.

In a short time, Mr. Lorry's coach was leaving the city.

You have your passes?
Yes.

Dr. Alexandre Manette; his daughter Lucie; a child Lucie; Mr. Lorry, banker, English; Sydney Carton, English—Mr. Carton is not well?

He will recover in the fresh air.

The coach passed through in safety.

Depart, citizens!

In the meantime, Madame Defarge made plans of her own.

Evremonde dies today, but his wife and child still live. Are they not also Evremondes?
Yes! They too must die.

I will go to them now to find them crying over the death of Evremonde. That too is a crime, you know. . . .
. . . .and punishable by death.

Alone in the apartment, Miss Pross was getting ready to follow her dear friends in another coach, when Madame Defarge appeared at the door.

The wife and child of Evremonde; where are they?
If only I can give my darlings some more time to get out of Paris.

You shall not see them as long as I can stop you, you evil woman!
Idiot! Let me by!

From the folds of her skirt, Madame Defarge drew a pistol. They fought briefly, and. . . .

A few minutes later, Miss Pross was on her way out of Paris.

As Lucie, Charles, and the others made their way back to England, Sydney Carton was on his way to the Guillotine.

You are not Evremonde! Why do you die for him?
For his wife and child.

If he could have written his thoughts, Sydney Carton would have said: "I see a beautiful city and beautiful people rising from the evil of this time. In England, I see the lives for which I lay down my life, peaceful, and happy. I see myself held in memory in their hearts, and honored in their souls."

They said that night, that his was the most peaceful face ever seen on that platform.

It is a far, far better thing that I do, than I have ever done; it is a far, far better rest that I go to, than I have ever known.

The End

WORDS TO KNOW

accused
beheaded
emigrant
exile
revolution
treason
witness

QUESTIONS

1. Why were the people of France fighting a revolution?

2. What was Charles Darnay's real name?

3. Why did he refuse to use that name?

4. What does the word *emigrant* mean as it was used in this story?

5. Who killed the Marquis St. Evremonde?

6. Why had Dr. Manette been placed in jail?

7. Why would the story have ended differently if Dr. Manette had never been in jail?

8. Why did Madame DeFarge want the entire Darnay family killed off?

9. Why didn't Darnay complain when Carton took his place in jail?